T0195953

ELIZABETH FITZGERALD

DINNY BECOMES A HERO

AuthorHouse™ UK
1663 Liberty Drive
Bloomington, IN 47403 USA
www.authorhouse.co.uk
Phone: 0800 047 8203 (Domestic TFN)
        +44 1908 723714 (International)

Published by AuthorHouse 09/28/2019

ISBN: 978-1-7283-9426-8 (sc)
ISBN: 978-1-7283-9425-1 (e)

Print information available on the last page.

This book is printed on acid-free paper.

DINNY BECOMES A HERO

authorHOUSE®

It was 7 o'clock and the start of a new day. Dinny woke most mornings at this time due to the sun shining brightly through the light curtains and the muffling sounds that came from the industrial estate straight through the window.

Dinny was almost 8 years old, however due to his small structure, to the eye, he looked no more than five or six. Along with this, Dinny had a stammer. He found it hard to talk to others. Not because He was stupid or ignorant, actually the opposite he was very bright, "our little Einstein" his mother often called him. When uncle Paddy would call and talk about the horses and fairs Dinny always knew which fair and what pony was bought. He could recall each marking on both horse and sulky.

His stammer was caused by the fact he had so much to say but he never knew where to begin. Oddly it only happened when he was a bit nervous speaking among strangers which made made him feel sad and embarrassed he longed for the ability of fluency in his speech.

Dinny is part of the traveling community and before he went to school he had many jobs to do. He has a five-year-old pony called Misty. She was tied up to a pole beside the family caravan that was in a field, behind an industrial state. He has to feed her nuts and give her a new bit of land to graze each morning. Dinny enjoyed this as Misty was his best friend. Dinny told Misty all his secrets and played with her every morning and evening. After brushing her, which he loved to do, he would put on her bridle and harness and attach her to the sulky. Dinny felt he was free from everyone and everything when he went trotting around the area where he lived with Misty on the sulky.

This caravan was the best they had ever seen. The inside was so grand with its red leather upholstery that shone like a polished apple, fluffy white carpet covered the floor. There were big sweet smelling flowers along with Ornaments that filled the shelves, they had a TV which slid out from the ceiling with a DVD player. They even had a computer it was built into another compartment. The kitchen area had a fridge that was filled with all sorts of food and drink. Each morning his mother would boil the kettle on the cooker for hot water so as he could wash himself in preparation for school but unlike his sisters he didn't have long hair so washing time was quick.

Dinny has four brothers and two sisters who walked into school every day. He likes school but he found it hard to keep up with all the other children in his class. His teacher Miss Murphy, was a young woman who always seemed to trot about. Everyday she wore a grey two-piece suit, black or white shirt with a tight skirt which forced her to make quick little steps. She always smiled gracefully but there was a stern look about her that reminded Dinny of his older sister when she would tell him it was time for bed.

Dinny hated wearing his school uniform, his collar rubbing off his neck, as for the tie, its only purpose was to choke him. His shoes rubbing off his heal making it impossible to sit still in class.

He looked forward to hearing miss Murphy reading stories to the class.

Dinny loved to read, but writing like speaking was difficult and frustrating, it was as if his hand could not keep up with his brain when he was writing. When he told Miss Murphy this, she would say, "Try harder Dinny," but it seemed illegible when he wrote quickly. Some days Miss Murphy would give Dinny jobs to do, he was first with his hand up for the opportunity to visit Mr. O'Grady who was the school principal. He always listened to Dinny's stories about his horses and the fairs with great intent.

Whoever he sat beside in class would ignore him and would never let him borrow as much as a pencil. Dinny felt lonely in the classroom, he spent most of his time gazing out of the window which overlooks a Broad lawn sloping down gently to an enormous beach tree that obscured his view of the road. Nobody wanted to pair with Dinny when it was time to do arts and crafts or PE. At lunchtime the other boys in the class would never let him join in any of the games so Mikey always brought his bag of colored Marbles to school so that he could play with them at break times.

One day when Dinny was playing with his marbles a boy called Barry from his class came up to him and asked him if he'd like to play soccer. Dinny didn't know much about Soccer, but he was so fed up of being alone, he decided to take desperate measures knowing quite well the only game he ever played with a ball was bowls,which are played only in the evenings throwing the ball down a long stretch of road which he did with his father and brothers. Not wanting to refuse the chance of a friend he said yes to the soccer match. Barry was surprised Dinny had never played soccer before. Dinny explained he had a pony called Misty, the conversation continued, Dinny explaining everything there is to know about horses, ponies, mares, foals, piebalds, skewbalds and cobs. Giving a picturesque description of a sulky, how to jock a horse and trot. Barry was excited about going for a spin on Dinny's sulky.

Barry decided it was time to play a real game of soccer, he approached a group of boys to request a challenge match. Dinny thought without a shadow of doubt this six or seven certified misfits, who Dinny used to see when out trotting,spent the weekends hanging around the streets kicking balls off walls were sure to win. A Fighting bunch, especially the leader the black haired, hatched faced with deep blue eyes, Paul is his name. He always wore a long sleeved see through coat over his uniform at the slightest hint of rain.They obviously derived a huge amount of fun from their game as they were always boasting about the matches excitedly amongst themselves, seemingly immune from the jeers that came from others around them.

Dinny knew he needed to put a lot of effort into this match he was excited at first to show off his skill. The test with simple he had to run with the ball passing it to Barry and score a goal. There was a lot at stake the honour of becoming a part of the group and a soccer player. The test was simple on the approach to the goal shooting on target in range and score a goal. Dinny had to compete with the great Paul him self and four others. He was so eager that he went completely wild, shooting at the goalkeeper and running up and down the field he became so engrossed in the game that he forgot to pass the ball to the other boys. During half time in the game Dinny asked his goalkeeper, "How are we doing?" He cheerfully answers "three goals Dinny" "and Paul's team" "nil" replied the goalkeeper. Dinny was beaming surly he thought to himself I must have passed the test. The bell rings.

Only then did he notice the grumpy faces around him. In one fell scoop he had turned his new friends to be into mortal enemies. They left without a word. Dinny looked at Barry for answers as to what he had done wrong. Barry explained "you must pass the ball around so everyone gets a chance to kick the ball".

Shortly after, the boys started to ask Barry, why he was playing with a traveller when he himself wasn't one. Barry didn't want to stop playing with Dinny but when his friend started ignoring him he had to consider if he wanted to remain friends with Dinny and risk being left out of all the lunchtime activity himself.

The next day at lunchtime Dinny was waiting for Barry, but after a few minutes past he realized that Barry had gone off playing soccer with the other boys in his class. Dinny felt so sad he could not bear this felling, as for these last few days he had tossed emotions of both joy and delight. But the anger he felt now was no match for this enormous grief. Tears were never far away, he had to do something, his best friend was gone, but how? But why? Sad and alone Dinny returned to his usual corner and began playing with his marbles, waiting for the bell to ring so as he could return to the classroom or better return home to his one and true friend Misty.

Every now and again Barry caught a glimpse of Dinny playing alone in the yard but decided to continue playing soccer with his classmates.

Early one morning in later November Dinny and his siblings were getting ready to venture out into the streets. He didn't relish the prospect, but he knew he had no choice as he had to go to school. The snow was falling at a steady pace now and soon the little town would have its own white blanket. On his arrival at school, Dinny notice all the children slipping and sliding around the yard cheering whomever slid the furthest. All of a sudden there were children scampering everywhere shouting for teachers "Barry is hurt", "Barry is after falling he can't get up". Dinny upon hearing these words ran immediately to see who is hurt? Could this be his friend Barry, looking through the sea of children Dinny caught a glimpse of Barry lying on the ground his leg distorted, Stuck as if frozen Dinny was in shock feeling he was apart from the others in a glass bubble, separate in shock, his friend Barry

Dinny began to think what can I do how can I help!

Just then some pushing and shoving erupted behind him the principal joined the big group of children who had gathered around Barry.Mr O'Grady was a big meaty man with a large stature and stood sweating profusely in his shirt and tie with his jacket draped across his arm. He was talking aloud, frantically to the other teachers in the yard, the realization that Barry needed to go to the hospital, he needed help immediately.

After trying for 10 minutes to get a car out of the car park the teachers didn't know what to do how were they going to get Barry to the hospital? Dinny tried to collect his thoughts but found it hard to think with all this talking, pushing and shoving. The teachers by now were getting impatient, bad tempered and shouting aloud at the children to stop sliding on the ice. Dinny desperately wanting to say something, but he would probably only stutter, or end up having everyone looking at him or worse laughing at him. The next moment without realizing Dinny shouted I.I.I can help!

The whole yard fell silent to gaze at Dinny, several grinned mockingly,only Mr O'Grady looked at him with interest.The others made him nervous and his next sentence come out I I I, I said t.T.T he went, turning Scarlett.. When someone sniggered he couldn't take it any longer he turned round and ran away, unthinkingly in the wrong direction. As he turned to change his direction for home standing in front of him was Mr. O Grady "Where are you going to Dinny?" exclaimed Mr. O'Grady. "I can help sir, I can help" stuttered Dinny. "How can you help Dinny? How can you help?" questioned Mr O Grady. "Misty can travel in the snow sir I know she can, I know she can. We can get Barry to the hospital quickly" Dinny replied confidently.

On Dinnys return with Misty and the sulky the teachers were in despair but they had no other option but to agree for Dinny to take Barry to the hospital. All the children were cheering Dinny on as Misty trotted down the road with Barry.At the hospital the doctors give Barry an x-ray and discovered his leg was broken they put his leg in a cast, gave him some crutches and sent them on their way *schoolword bound.*

He had done it, Dinny had done it, as by magic all the tension, all the anger and all that frustration vanished, they just evaporated. He threw his arms around misty and began to weep but they were tears of joy, thank you Misty I knew you could do it". Happily he punched the air as he was totally delighted his best friend was safe. Barry turned to Dinny, "I'm sorry Dinny you are a true friend." Dinny looked at Barry and said "I did promise you a spin in my sulky" the two boys laughed.

On their return to the school the teachers and Barry's parents were standing at the school gate awaiting their arrival. Barry's parents thanked Dinny for taking their son to the hospital. Dinny jumped up onto the back of the sulky and started to walk out the school gate. Mr O Grady stopped Dinny at the gate, he stretched out his hand and patted Dinny on the head "don't you worry lad you did a great job" Dinny could not believe his ears and smile back at Mr O'Grady. "All the other children have gone home due to the snow we will see you back here again on Monday Dinny take care of misty" continued Mr O'Grady.

On Monday at school all the children were talking about how Dinny was a hero and asked him to tell them all about the visit to the hospital. Barry told them how exciting it was to go on Dinnys sulky. Barry asked Dinny to sign his cast handing him a black permanent marker, each of the children lined up for the opportunity to sign also. Dinny was delighted and now every day at school Dinny sits beside his friend Barry and at lunchtime they play soccer with Paul and all of his other classmates..

The author of this book full name is Elizabeth Fitzgerald who lives in co. cork, Ireland. She is a widow with four children. She return to collage at the age of thirty four where she studied English literature as part of her Bachelor of Arts Degree in Montessori. During her final year of her degree she wrote this book as part of her module.

After serval years of hiding away in a box and a lot of persuading by her children who believed she should share this story with others. Elizabeth took the necessary steps and here it is.

Personal note from the author:

"I really hope you enjoy reading this book as much as my children".

Elizabeth Fitzgerald

Printed in the United States
By Bookmasters